Investments

Creating the Strategy

By

Dr. David K. Ewen

ISBN: 9798870012803

Imprint: Independently published by Enterprise College

Cover Art by Joshua Mayo via Unsplash

About the Book

The book emphasizes that comprehending profitable investment opportunities plays a crucial role in achieving financial success. It stresses the significance of an individual's risk tolerance, financial aspirations, and personal principles as fundamental elements in successful investing.

According to the book, succeeding in the realm of investments requires a meticulous approach involving thorough research, occasional expert advice, and a strategic allocation of investments to minimize risks.

It highlights that every investment avenue comes with its own set of risks and rewards, necessitating individuals to formulate a well-informed investment strategy aligned with their specific goals and circumstances. This strategy, as per the book, should integrate prudent decision-making with a comprehensive understanding of the investment landscape.

About the Author

Dr. David K. Ewen embarked on his inaugural significant investment journey by founding his company in 1994. Over time, this venture has evolved into a global enterprise, affording him a comprehensive insight into investment strategies within the context of a global economy.

Dr. Ewen's journey from an entrepreneur launching a company to overseeing its growth into a global entity has likely provided Dr. Ewen with invaluable insights into the complexities of international markets, diverse investment opportunities, and the significance of adapting investment strategies in response to global economic trends.

Table of Contents

Dr. David K. Ewen

Chapter 1: Introduction

Building financial stability and achieving long-term goals are crucial in today's fast-paced world. The art of investing wisely plays a pivotal role in this endeavor. As we navigate through a sea of investment options, it becomes increasingly important to make informed decisions about where to allocate our financial resources. But remember, there is no one-size-fits-all approach to investing.

To embark on this financial journey, we must first grasp a comprehensive understanding of the diverse investment vehicles at our disposal. From stocks to bonds, mutual funds to real estate, and even commodities like gold and oil, each option presents its own unique advantages and risks. It's like exploring a vast landscape of opportunities, where only the knowledgeable thrive.

Let's take a closer look at some of these options. Stocks, for instance, offer the tantalizing potential for high returns, but they dance hand in hand with the ever-volatile market. On the other hand, bonds, often considered a safer choice, may yield lower returns. Mutual funds, however, provide a brilliant avenue for diversification, pooling resources from multiple investors and creating a well-rounded portfolio. Real estate investments can bring forth steady income through rental properties or appreciate in value over time. And then there are commodities, the wildcards of the investment world. They promise the chance of significant returns but can be as unpredictable as a summer storm.

But don't venture into these investment landscapes unprepared. Thorough research and seeking professional advice are essential to make the right decisions. Understanding your own risk tolerance is key as well. Some may embrace the thrill of high-risk investments, chasing after greater returns. Others may prefer a more cautious approach, gravitating towards conservative options. Regardless, maintaining a long-term perspective and resisting the temptation to succumb to short-term market fluctuations is paramount.

To navigate the choppy waters of investment, diversification is your compass. By spreading your investments across different asset classes, you can mitigate risks and optimize returns. Remember, it's not about putting all your eggs in one basket; it's about creating a sturdy financial safety net.

Lastly, staying on track towards your financial goals requires regular portfolio reviews and adjustments. The investment landscape is ever-evolving, and your strategies must adapt accordingly. Flexibility is the key to success.

Making wise investment decisions is a multifaceted endeavor that necessitates thoughtful consideration of numerous factors. Understanding the diverse opportunities and potential risks inherent in each investment option empowers individuals to make informed choices that harmonize with their financial objectives. So, venture into this dynamic world equipped with knowledge, and pave the path towards establishing financial stability and realizing your long-term aspirations.

Investing wisely involves a comprehensive evaluation of various investment avenues available in the market. From stocks, bonds, and mutual funds to real estate, commodities, and alternative investments, each option carries its own set of risks, potential returns, and market dynamics. It's crucial to delve into these intricacies, assessing how each investment aligns with your goals, risk tolerance, and time horizon.

Furthermore, conducting thorough research is fundamental. This encompasses analyzing historical performance, understanding market trends, studying economic indicators, and keeping abreast of global events that could impact investment markets. By gathering and evaluating relevant information, investors can make informed decisions, minimizing uncertainties and potential pitfalls.

Risk management forms a critical component of wise investing. Different investments carry varying degrees of risk. While some options might promise higher returns, they often come with increased volatility and uncertainty. Conversely, more conservative investments might offer stability but with potentially lower returns. Balancing risk and return is key, and diversification across multiple asset classes can mitigate overall portfolio risk.

Aligning investments with long-term financial objectives is essential. Investing isn't merely about short-term gains but about laying the groundwork for future financial security and meeting life goals. Whether it's saving for retirement, funding education, or building wealth, having a clear roadmap guides investment decisions in a direction that supports these aspirations.

Seeking guidance from financial advisors or experts can be invaluable. Their expertise can offer insights and guidance tailored to individual circumstances, helping navigate the complexities of the investment landscape and steering towards well-informed decisions.

Ultimately, stepping into the world of investing armed with knowledge and a strategic approach enhances the potential for success. Embracing the multifaceted nature of investment decisions, understanding the opportunities, assessing risks, and aligning choices with long-term goals empowers individuals to build a robust financial foundation. It's a journey that demands continuous learning, adaptability, and a prudent approach, ultimately paving the way for financial stability and the realization of long-cherished aspirations.

Chapter 2: Stock Market

Investing in stocks opens a world of possibilities, where individuals can become partial owners of companies and potentially unlock financial rewards. It's like stepping into the driver's seat of your financial future. Picture this: when a company thrives, its stock values soar, paving the way for investors to cash in on their brilliant choices. But, let's not forget, the stock market is a wild and unpredictable beast. That's why diving into comprehensive research and analysis is the secret sauce that separates the winners from the rest.

To truly grasp the potential of any investment, it's crucial to understand the inner workings of a company. Peering into its financial health, industry dynamics, and market trends offers a glimpse into its growth prospects and profitability. It's like peeling back the layers of a juicy financial onion. And how do you do that? By digging into financial statements like balance sheets, income statements, and cash flow statements. These little nuggets hold the key to evaluating a company's overall stability and performance.

But that's not all. Keeping your finger on the pulse of the company's industry is a must-do. It's like being a detective, always on the lookout for hidden opportunities or lurking risks that could sway the company's growth prospects. And let's not forget about market trends and investor sentiment. By analyzing these factors, investors can decode the overall market conditions and make smarter, more informed investment decisions.

Remember, don't put all your eggs in one basket. Diversification is the name of the game. By spreading your investments across different companies and sectors, you're reducing the risk of any single company's poor performance dragging down your entire portfolio. It's like building a fortress that can withstand any storm.

In the exhilarating realm of stocks, patience stands as a vital virtue. It's effortless to be swayed by the allure of rapid gains or the latest market fads. However, genuine success in investing stems from a commitment to diligent research, meticulous analysis, and a disciplined approach that focuses on the long-term horizon. So, gear up, fasten your seatbelt, and prepare yourself for an exhilarating journey toward financial growth and prosperity.

Stock markets are a dynamic landscape where fluctuations, trends, and volatility are part of the norm. Amidst this whirlwind, it's natural for investors to feel tempted by the promise of quick profits or the excitement of short-term trends. Yet, history has shown that lasting success in the stock market often belongs to those who practice patience and maintain a steadfast focus on long-term objectives.

The foundation of a successful stock market journey lies in thorough research and analysis. Understanding the fundamentals of companies, assessing their financial health, evaluating market trends, and comprehending the potential risks are essential steps before making investment decisions. This diligence allows investors to make informed choices based on solid data rather than fleeting market sentiments.

A disciplined approach to investing involves sticking to a well-thought-out investment strategy, even during turbulent market conditions. It includes setting clear goals, diversifying investments, and adhering to a predefined risk tolerance level. This discipline helps in avoiding emotional decisions driven by market fluctuations, ensuring a more rational and measured approach to investing.

Moreover, embracing a long-term perspective is paramount. The stock market is a marathon, not a sprint. Patiently weathering market fluctuations, holding onto quality investments, and allowing time for compound interest to work its magic can lead to substantial growth and wealth accumulation over the years.

Additionally, maintaining a diversified portfolio can help cushion against market volatility.

Spreading investments across different sectors, industries, or asset classes can mitigate risks and enhance the potential for consistent returns over time.

So, buckle in for the ride! Embrace the excitement of the stock market while being mindful of the need for patience, diligence, and a long-term perspective. By staying grounded, conducting thorough research, and adhering to a disciplined investment strategy, investors can navigate the twists and turns of the market with confidence, positioning themselves for enduring financial growth and prosperity.

Chapter 3: Real Estate

Embark on an exciting financial journey with real estate investment—a strategic move that involves acquiring properties to generate rental income or witness their value appreciate over time. This long-term investment strategy has captivated individuals seeking stability and a steady stream of income. One of the greatest perks of real estate investment lies in the potential for regular rental income, which gracefully supplements other sources and ensures a consistent cash flow. Moreover, real estate has a remarkable track record of appreciating in value over the years, offering investors the chance to reap substantial rewards from their initial investment.

However, it's worth noting that real estate investment demands a substantial amount of capital to get started. Property prices vary greatly, influenced by factors such as location, size, and condition. As a savvy investor, you need to be prepared to make significant financial commitments. Additionally, ongoing maintenance costs can accumulate, as properties require regular upkeep and occasional repairs. It's essential to allocate a budget for these expenses to safeguard the profitability of your investment.

Furthermore, real estate investment necessitates a deep understanding of the market and thorough research. Familiarizing yourself with the local real estate landscape, including trends, demographics, and rental demand, is crucial for making informed investment decisions. By arming yourself with this knowledge, you can confidently navigate the market and seize opportunities that align with your goals.

In summary, the realm of real estate investment holds the allure of stability, potential income, and long-term growth. However, for investors eyeing this promising domain, it is crucial to undertake thorough analysis, consider the financial implications, ongoing expenses, and be mindful of market dynamics before delving into this potentially rewarding venture. With a strategic and informed approach, real estate investment has the potential to unlock a myriad of opportunities and become a cornerstone of your financial success.

Real estate investment offers unique advantages such as a tangible asset, potential for rental income, and the possibility of appreciation over time. However, it's imperative to approach it with prudence and foresight. Understanding the financial implications, including upfront costs, ongoing expenses like maintenance, property taxes, insurance, and potential vacancy periods is essential. Conducting meticulous market research to grasp local real estate trends, demand-supply dynamics, and economic conditions is crucial before making investment decisions.

Moreover, the financing aspect of real estate investments demands careful consideration. Assessing mortgage options, interest rates, and the potential impact on cash flow is pivotal in making sound investment choices. It's prudent to weigh the risks against potential returns, factoring in both short-term gains and long-term appreciation.

Furthermore, being aware of the different avenues within real estate—residential, commercial, industrial, or development projects—allows investors to align their investment strategy with their financial goals and risk tolerance. Each sector carries its own set of opportunities and risks, necessitating a tailored approach to suit individual preferences and objectives.

Despite the potential rewards, real estate investment demands active management and commitment. It requires vigilance in property maintenance, tenant management (if applicable), and staying abreast of market fluctuations. Engaging with professionals such as real estate agents, property managers, or financial advisors can provide valuable insights and guidance throughout the investment journey.

Ultimately, with careful planning, due diligence, and a long-term perspective, real estate investment can be a formidable asset in a diversified investment portfolio. It has the potential to generate steady income, build wealth over time, and serve as a stable foundation for financial security. By approaching real estate investment with caution, leveraging market knowledge, and a sound investment strategy, investors can harness its potential to create a robust and prosperous financial future.

Chapter 4: Mutual Funds and ETFs

Mutual Funds and Exchange-Traded Funds (ETFs) have become incredibly popular investment options, allowing individuals to step into the world of diversified portfolios. Instead of going solo, these investment vehicles pool money from multiple investors and allocate it across a variety of assets like stocks, bonds, and commodities. This means investors get exposure to a wide range of investments and enjoy the benefits of diversification, which can lead to more stable returns compared to individual stock investments.

Investing in Mutual Funds or ETFs opens the door to a professionally managed portfolio. Experienced fund managers take the reins, making sound investment decisions on behalf of the investors. These managers dig deep into research and analysis, seeking out the most attractive investment opportunities that align with the fund's investment mandate. By tapping into their expertise, even investors with limited knowledge or time can benefit from the wisdom and skills of these professionals.

Diversification is a key advantage of Mutual Funds and ETFs. It's like spreading your investment wings across different asset classes, sectors, and regions to minimize risks. Picture this: if one stock within your Mutual Fund or ETF takes a hit, the overall impact on your portfolio is cushioned by the positive performance of other investments within the fund. It's an excellent way to protect yourself against the unpredictability of individual investments.

But it doesn't stop there. By coming together in Mutual Funds and ETFs, investors gain access to a world of investment opportunities that might otherwise be out of reach. With substantial assets under management, these investment vehicles have the power to invest in various assets. They can dip their toes in international stocks, bonds, real estate investment trusts (REITs), or even commodities, giving investors a taste of different markets and asset classes.

What's more, Mutual Funds and ETFs offer investors a high level of liquidity. Unlike investing in individual stocks or other assets, you can easily buy or sell your shares on an exchange. This flexibility means you can swiftly enter or exit your positions, making investing a breeze.

And here's the cherry on top: Mutual Funds and ETFs often have lower investment minimums compared to directly purchasing individual stocks or other assets. This means a wider range of investors, including those with limited capital, can get in on the action. The barriers to entry are lowered, allowing everyone to participate in the financial markets and pursue their investment goals.

Whether you're an experienced investor or taking your first steps into the world of investing, Mutual Funds and Exchange-Traded Funds (ETFs) serve as your gateway to building a diversified investment portfolio. They present an opportunity to combine resources, access a multitude of assets, and potentially secure more consistent returns. With their professional management, liquidity, and lower investment minimums, these investment vehicles offer a convenient and accessible route to financial success.

Mutual Funds and ETFs act as effective tools for diversification. They enable investors to spread their investments across various asset classes, such as stocks, bonds, commodities, and real estate, without needing to individually select and manage each investment. This diversification helps mitigate risks by reducing the impact of volatility in any single asset.

Professional management is a key feature of Mutual Funds and ETFs. Skilled fund managers oversee the portfolio, conducting research, making investment decisions, and rebalancing the holdings to align with the fund's objectives. This expertise adds a layer of confidence for investors, especially those who may not have the time or expertise to manage investments actively.

Furthermore, both Mutual Funds and ETFs offer liquidity, allowing investors to buy or sell shares easily on stock exchanges at market prices. This liquidity ensures that investors can access their funds when needed, providing a level of flexibility and convenience.

Compared to investing directly in individual stocks or bonds, Mutual Funds and ETFs typically have lower investment minimums, making them more accessible to a broader range of investors. This accessibility enables individuals with varying financial capacities to participate in the markets and benefit from professional management and diversified exposure.

ETFs, in particular, have additional advantages such as intra-day trading flexibility and lower expense ratios due to their passive management style, tracking a market index's performance.

Both Mutual Funds and ETFs offer investors the chance to potentially achieve more stable returns over time, given their diversified nature and professional oversight. This stability can be particularly appealing to investors seeking a balanced and less volatile investment strategy.

In summary, whether you're a seasoned investor seeking diversification or someone starting their investment journey, Mutual Funds and ETFs serve as efficient vehicles. Their features of diversification, professional management, liquidity, and accessibility make them appealing options for building a well-rounded investment portfolio aimed at long-term financial success.

Chapter 5: Impact Investing

Are you passionate about investing in a better future? Look no further than impact investing! It's not your typical investment strategy. Impact investing goes beyond the traditional pursuit of financial gains. It's all about putting your money where your heart is and supporting companies and projects that aim to make a positive difference in the world.

Imagine being able to align your investment portfolio with your personal values and beliefs. Impact investing allows you to do just that. Whether you're passionate about renewable energy, gender equality, or improving education, you have the power to make a tangible impact in the areas that matter most to you.

But don't worry, impact investing isn't just about doing good—it can also be good for your wallet. Evidence shows that companies with strong environmental, social, and governance practices can actually deliver competitive financial returns. So, while you're making a difference, you can also potentially earn profits.

Impact investing isn't just about making money or supporting causes. It plays a crucial role in driving innovation and addressing pressing global challenges. By investing in companies and projects that tackle issues like climate change, poverty alleviation, and healthcare access, you become a catalyst for positive change. You're not just an investor, but an agent of progress.

Of course, impact investing isn't without its challenges. Assessing the social or environmental impact of investments can be complex, and finding the right opportunities that align with your impact goals can be daunting. But fear not! The growing interest in impact investing has led to the development of frameworks, standards, and tools to help you navigate these challenges and make informed decisions.

In conclusion, impact investing transcends being merely an investment strategy; it embodies a profound means to foster a better world. It empowers individuals to effect positive change while potentially reaping financial returns. Why not become part of this transformative movement? With accessible resources and expertise at hand, impact invocting etande ae an inviting and feasible option for anyone seeking to create a meaningful difference through their investments. The time is now to commence investing in a brighter future!

Impact investing isn't solely about financial gains; it's a deliberate effort to channel capital into projects, companies, or initiatives that generate positive social or environmental outcomes alongside potential profitability. By aligning investment decisions with values and objectives, impact investors wield their financial power to drive change in areas such as sustainability, social justice, healthcare, education, and beyond.

The beauty of impact investing lies in its accessibility. It caters to a wide spectrum of investors, from seasoned professionals to those starting their investment journey. Diverse platforms, funds, and investment opportunities exist, catering to varying interests and causes. This accessibility ensures that anyone with the desire to contribute to a better world can do so through their investment choices.

Moreover, impact investing doesn't demand sacrificing financial returns for the sake of making a positive difference. Instead, it seeks to harness the synergy between social or environmental impact and financial gain. This dual-purpose approach resonates with a growing number of investors who prioritize creating meaningful change without compromising their financial goals.

The momentum behind impact investing continues to surge, fueled by a global shift toward sustainability and social responsibility. Governments, corporations, and individuals are recognizing the immense potential of investments that generate positive impacts while bolstering financial portfolios.

So, why not seize the opportunity to be part of this movement? By embracing impact investing, you join a community of changemakers who believe in leveraging capital for the greater good. Whether you're passionate about environmental conservation, social equality, or other causes, impact investing offers a way to align your values with your investment decisions.

With readily available resources, expert guidance, and an array of impactful investment avenues, now is the time to embark on this transformative journey. Start shaping a brighter future today by investing not just in financial returns but in positive change, knowing that each investment made has the potential to create a world that is more equitable, sustainable, and prosperous for all.

Chapter 6: Self-Investment

Embarking on a journey of personal growth, education, skills, or entrepreneurship holds the key to unlocking a multitude of rewards in every facet of life. It's not just about boosting our knowledge and abilities; it's about amplifying our earning potential and embracing exciting new prospects. In fact, the value of investing our time, effort, and resources into self-development can rival, if not surpass, the gains made from financial investments.

As we proactively seek to broaden our horizons and sharpen our skills, we empower ourselves to navigate the ever-evolving landscape of the world and surge ahead in remarkable ways. Education, in particular, wields immense power to equip us with the tools needed to navigate the intricate workings of the modern workforce. Whether we pursue a formal education or embark on a self-directed learning journey, investing in education lays a sturdy foundation for personal and professional growth.

Moreover, acquiring new skills or honing existing ones can be a game-changer for our employability and earning potential. The continuous pursuit of learning and skill development ensures that we remain competitive in the job market and secure a coveted edge. By seizing opportunities to expand our skill set, we solidify our position and pave the way for prosperity.

Venturing into the realm of entrepreneurship, on the other hand, can be a transformative odyssey that not only brings financial rewards but also nourishes our souls with personal fulfillment. It encourages us to take daring risks, foster creative thinking, and seize the untapped potential that surrounds us. Through entrepreneurship, we bring our passions to life, crafting something meaningful while making meaningful contributions to both the economy and society at large.

Ultimately, channeling our resources into personal growth, education, skill development, or entrepreneurship stands as an investment of unparalleled value. This commitment yields remarkable dividends, offering an expansive reservoir of knowledge, limitless prospects, and a life adorned with fulfillment and prosperity. Let us wholeheartedly embrace this odyssey of self-investment, where each stride forward propels us toward a future adorned with triumph, contentment, and boundless possibilities.

Investing in oneself and nurturing personal growth is akin to cultivating a flourishing garden. It involves dedicating time and energy to expand one's knowledge, refine skills, and foster a mindset conducive to constant evolution. By investing in education, whether formal or informal, we acquire the tools necessary to navigate life's complexities and unlock our true potential. Education broadens horizons, enabling us to view the world through a lens of understanding and enlightenment.

Moreover, honing skills or venturing into entrepreneurship is an embodiment of self-investment. It involves taking calculated risks, embracing challenges, and fostering innovation. Skills acquired through dedication and practice not only enrich our capabilities but also open doors to a myriad of opportunities in various professional spheres.

Similarly, entrepreneurship nurtures a spirit of creativity and resilience, offering a path towards self-reliance and the creation of meaningful contributions to society.

This journey of self-investment is not solely about tangible gains; it is also about the intangible riches that enrich our lives. It cultivates resilience, adaptability, and a growth-oriented mindset that transcends mere material wealth. It fosters a sense of fulfillment derived from personal achievements, contributing to a life steeped in satisfaction and purpose.

Each step taken in this pursuit of self-investment is a step toward a future shimmering with success and fulfillment. It is a testament to our commitment to continuous improvement and the realization of our aspirations. Every lesson learned, skill acquired, or entrepreneurial endeavor undertaken paves the way for a life brimming with opportunities waiting to be seized.

So, let us embark on this transformative journey of self-investment with zeal and determination. Let us embrace the challenges and relish the triumphs, for each milestone reached brings us closer to a future where success, contentment, and limitless possibilities abound. This journey isn't merely about reaching a destination; it's about savoring the growth, the experiences, and the evolution that unfolds along the way.

Chapter 7: Real Estate Investment Trust

Experience the wealth-building potential of Real Estate Investment Trusts (REITs), a captivating and secure long-term investment strategy. REITs are the powerhouses that own and manage profit-generating properties, ranging from bustling office buildings and bustling shopping malls to cozy apartments and luxurious hotels. By delving into REITs, you can effortlessly tap into the real estate market without the hassle of property ownership and management.

Prepare to be enchanted by the enchanting advantages of investing in REITs. Firstly, revel in the consistent flow of income that REITs offer. These magical entities are bound by law to share a significant portion of their taxable income with shareholders as enticing dividends. Picture yourself basking in the glow of a steady stream of passive income.

But the magic doesn't stop there. Brace yourself for the enchantment of diversification. REITs possess the ability to spread their investment spells across various properties in different sectors and geographic locations. This spellbinding feat reduces the risk that comes with having all your real estate eggs in one basket. As if that weren't enough, REITs often perform their enchantments on public exchanges, offering investors the liquid magic of easily buying and selling shares.

And now, prepare to be transported to a realm where the value of your investments can soar. As the properties owned by these mystical REITs increase in value, the market price of their shares can ascend to new heights. Imagine reaping the rewards of capital appreciation as your investments flourish and prosper.

But, like any magical journey, investing in REITs also carries risks. The value of these enchanting shares can fluctuate, potentially leading to losses. Changes in interest rates, economic conditions, or the real estate market itself can cast a shadow on the performance of REITs. Hence, it is essential to embark on thorough research, analyzing the financial health, management prowess, and track record of the REIT before embarking on this magical investment quest.

In conclusion, invite Real Estate Investment Trusts (REITs) to wield their enchantment within your investment portfolio, bestowing upon you the mesmerizing advantages of diversification, steady income generation, and entrance into the captivating realm of real estate. Yet, heed that this mystical journey demands thoughtful contemplation and dedicated study. Are you prepared to unravel the mysteries of REITs and partake in the enchantment they present?

REITs, like magical conduits, offer investors access to the real estate market without direct ownership of properties. They weave spells of diversification by spreading investments across various real estate sectors like commercial properties, residential buildings, healthcare facilities, and more. This diversification acts as a shield, guarding against the volatility that might besiege individual properties.

Moreover, these magical entities have the ability to generate regular income through dividends. By law, REITs distribute a significant portion of their earnings to shareholders, offering an enticing source of consistent cash flow for investors seeking regular income streams.

Stepping into the captivating world of real estate through REITs also provides a unique vantage point. It grants a stake in the real estate market's potential appreciation and growth, allowing participation in the fortunes of this tangible asset class without the burdens of property management.

However, navigating this magical journey necessitates caution and a willingness to delve into the intricacies of REIT investments. Understanding the nuances of different types of REITs, their management styles, the sectors they operate in, and their performance trends is crucial. It's akin to studying the various enchantments in a spellbook before casting a magical incantation.

Furthermore, market conditions and economic fluctuations can influence the performance of REITs, adding an element of unpredictability to this mystical landscape. Diligent research, ongoing monitoring, and a balanced approach are essential to harnessing the potential benefits while mitigating risks.

So, are you prepared to embark on this magical odyssey? Are you willing to unearth the secrets of REITs, aligning your investment goals with the captivating opportunities they offer? The spellbinding benefits of diversification, income generation, and exposure to the enchanting realm of real estate await those who are ready to embrace the journey.

Chapter 8: Education as the Best Investment

Imagine embarking on a transformative journey that not only equips you with knowledge, but also empowers you to succeed in life's diverse arenas. This is the power of education, widely regarded as the ultimate investment one can make in a lifetime.

Education goes beyond a mere accumulation of facts and figures. It is a catalyst for personal growth, enabling individuals to pursue their passions, fulfill their potential, and leave a meaningful mark on society. The impact of education is far-reaching, positively affecting not just individuals, but also families, communities, and even nations.

In our rapidly changing world, where technology and globalization are reshaping industries and economies, education has become more crucial than ever. It cultivates adaptability, critical thinking, problem-solving skills, and creativity - indispensable tools for navigating complex challenges and seizing opportunities.

Moreover, education paves the path to social mobility, breaking the cycle of poverty and offering individuals the means to improve their socioeconomic status. It opens doors to better career prospects, higher income potential, and an enhanced quality of life.

But education is not a one-time event; it is a lifelong process. It encourages intellectual curiosity, enabling individuals to stay intellectually engaged, continuously learn, and remain relevant in our ever-evolving world.

Education also plays a pivotal role in fostering social cohesion and understanding. It nurtures empathy, tolerance, and respect for diversity, paving the way for a more inclusive and harmonious society.

Furthermore, education serves as a powerful catalyst for positive change and sustainable development. It empowers individuals to address societal issues, promote environmental stewardship, and contribute to building a more equitable and prosperous future for all.

In conclusion, education stands as an unequivocal pinnacle investment - not merely in terms of acquiring knowledge but as an investment in oneself, in the future, and in the broader advancement of society. The significance of education goes beyond the boundaries of personal development; it is the cornerstone of progress, innovation, and societal evolution.

Embracing education transcends the confines of formal schooling; it encompasses a lifelong commitment to learning, growth, and intellectual curiosity. By placing value on continuous education, individuals can unlock their full potential, broaden their horizons, and contribute meaningfully to their communities and the world at large.

Education serves as a catalyst for personal empowerment. It equips individuals with the tools, skills, and critical thinking capabilities necessary to navigate the complexities of modern life. Beyond academic prowess, education fosters creativity, resilience, adaptability, and a deeper understanding of diverse perspectives - qualities that are invaluable in an ever-changing world.

Moreover, an investment in education doesn't solely benefit the individual; it radiates outward, catalyzing positive change and progress on a societal level. Educated individuals are more likely to innovate, create solutions to pressing challenges, and contribute to economic growth and social development.

By fostering a culture of lifelong learning, we open doors to boundless possibilities. The synergy of diverse knowledge, experiences, and perspectives fuels innovation and drives positive change in every sphere of society - from science and technology to the arts, humanities, and beyond.

So, let us embark on this transformative journey together - a journey where the pursuit of knowledge knows no boundaries. Let us commit ourselves to embrace education, to continuously seek wisdom, and to empower ourselves and others. In doing so, we unleash the potential within us and collectively propel towards a brighter, more inclusive, and prosperous future for all.

The impact of education is profound and far-reaching. It is not merely an investment in oneself but a beacon of hope and progress for humanity. Let us recognize its immense value and strive to create a world where education is accessible, cherished, and celebrated as the key to unlocking a world of opportunities and possibilities.

Chapter 9: Conclusion

Understanding the dynamics of profitable investment opportunities is a cornerstone of financial success, contingent upon an individual's risk tolerance, financial aspirations, and personal values. The path to success in investing demands meticulous research, occasional expert guidance, and the strategic spread of investments to mitigate risks.

Every investment avenue carries its own blend of risks and rewards. Thus, it is imperative for individuals to craft a well-informed investment strategy that resonates with their distinct objectives and circumstances. This strategy should be a fusion of prudent decision-making and a comprehensive understanding of the investment landscape.

The importance of diversification cannot be overstated. Spreading investments across different asset classes, industries, or geographical regions can cushion against sudden market volatilities or downturns in specific sectors. It's akin to not placing all eggs in a single basket.

Furthermore, the landscape of financial markets is perpetually evolving. Regularly reassessing and fine-tuning one's investment portfolio is critical to ensure its alignment with evolving financial objectives and market dynamics. Flexibility and adaptability are key here, allowing investors to capitalize on emerging opportunities while minimizing exposure to potential downsides.

Seeking guidance from financial advisors or experts can be invaluable, especially when navigating complex or unfamiliar investment territories. Their insights and expertise can offer clarity amidst market noise, helping investors make informed decisions aligned with their long-term goals.

However, prudent investing goes beyond market analysis and technical know-how. It also involves aligning investments with personal values and ethics. Socially responsible investing (SRI) or Environmental, Social, and Governance (ESG) considerations are gaining prominence, allowing individuals to support causes they believe in while seeking financial gains.

Ultimately, achieving success in investing necessitates a balanced approach. Maximizing returns while managing risks effectively requires a nuanced understanding of various factors. The journey to making wise investment decisions involves a delicate interplay of risk assessment, market knowledge, adaptability, and a continual reassessment of one's financial blueprint.

In essence, grasping profitable investment opportunities demands a comprehensive understanding of personal circumstances, financial goals, and the ever-evolving market. A well-crafted investment strategy tailored to individual needs, backed by thorough research and periodic adjustments, forms the bedrock of a successful investment journey.

www.ingramcontent.com/pod-product-compliance
Lightning Source LLC
Chambersburg PA
CBHW060004300526
45794CB00003B/1080